D0555380

HOWARD BRENTON

Howard Brenton was born in Portsmouth in 1942. His many plays include *Christie in Love* (Portable Theatre, 1969); *Revenge* (Royal Court Theatre, 1969); *Magnificence* (Royal Court Theatre, 1973); *The Churchill Play* (Nottingham Playhouse, 1974, and twice revived by the RSC, 1978 and 1988); *Weapons of Happiness* (National Theatre, Evening Standard Award, 1976); *Epsom Downs* (Joint Stock Theatre, 1977); *Sore Throats* (RSC, 1978); *The Romans in Britain* (National Theatre, 1980); *Thirteenth Night* (RSC, 1981); *Bloody Poetry* (Foco Novo, 1984, and Royal Court Theatre, 1987); *The Genius* (1983), *Greenland* (1988) and *Berlin Bertie* (1992) all presented by the Royal Court; *In Extremis* (University of California, 1997) and *Kit's Play* (RADA Jerwood Theatre, 2000).

Collaborations with other writers include *A Short Sharp Shock* (with Tony Howard, Royal Court and Stratford East, 1980); *Pravda* (with David Hare, National Theatre, Evening Standard Award, 1985); *Iranian Nights* (with Tariq Ali, Royal Court Theatre, 1989); *Moscow Gold* (with Tariq Ali, RSC, 1990); *Ugly Rumours* (with Tariq Ali, Tricycle Theatre, 1998); *Collateral Damage* (Tricycle Theatre, 1999) and *Snogging Ken* (Almeida Theatre, 2000), both with Tariq Ali and Andy de la Tour.

He wrote the libretto for Ben Mason's football opera *Playing Away* (Opera North and Munich Biennale, 1994) and a radio play, *Nasser's Eden* (1998). Versions of classics include *The Life of Galileo* (1980) and *Danton's Death* (1982) both for the National Theatre, and Goethe's *Faust* (1995/6) for the RSC.

His novel *Diving for Pearls* was published by Nick Hern Books in 1989. His book of essays on the theatre, *Hot Irons*, was published by Nick Hern Books (1995) and reissued, in an expanded paperback version, by Methuen (1998). He wrote thirteen episodes of the BBC1 drama series *Spooks* (2001-2005, BAFTA Best Drama Series 2003).

Other Titles in this Series

Howard Brenton

PAUL

NICK HERN BOOKS
London
www.nickhernbooks.co.uk

A Nick Hern Book

Paul first published in Great Britain as a paperback original in 2005 by Nick Hern Books Limited, 14 Larden Road, London W3 7ST

Corrected reprint 2006

Paul copyright © 2005 Howard Brenton

Cover design: Ned Hoste, 2H

Typeset by Country Setting, Kingsdown, Kent CT14 8ES
Printed in Great Britain by Cox and Wyman, Reading, Berks

A CIP catalogue record for this book is available from
the British Library

ISBN-13   978 1 85459 886 8
ISBN-10   1 85459 886 4

Paul was first performed in the Cottesloe auditorium of the National Theatre, London, on 9 November 2005 (previews from 1 November). The cast, in order of speaking, was as follows:

PAUL (at first SAUL)	Adam Godley
BARNABAS	Colin Tierney
YESHUA (Jesus)	Pearce Quigley
ARAB TRADER	Howard Saddler
PETER	Lloyd Owen
ROMAN GAOLER	Dermot Kerrigan
MARY MAGDALENE	Kellie Bright
JAMES	Paul Higgins
NERO	Richard Dillane
ENSEMBLE	Tas Emiabata
	Eugene Washington

Other parts played by members of the company

Director   Howard Davies
Designer   Vicki Mortimer
Lighting Designer   Paule Constable
Music   Dominic Muldowney
Sound Designer   John Leonard
Company Voice Work   Patsy Rodenburg

Assistant Director   Samantha Potter
Production Manager   Laurence Holderness
Stage Manager   Trish Montemuro
Deputy Stage Managers   Janice Heyes, Katy de Main
Assistant Stage Manager   Ben Wallace

PAUL

2

Characters

PAUL (*at first* SAUL)

BARNABAS

YESHUA (JESUS)

ARAB TRADER

ROMAN GAOLER

PETER

JAMES

MARY MAGDALENE

NERO

TEMPLE GUARDS, ROMAN GAOLERS,
CHRISTIANS AT CORINTH

*AD 36 to AD 65 in a Roman gaol, on the Damascus Road, in
Arabia, in James's house in Jerusalem, in Corinth.*

*This text went to press before the end of rehearsals so may
differ slightly from the play as performed.*

Scene One

Rome, AD 65. Prison. PAUL, aged 55, is in chains. He prays.

PAUL. Christ is risen. Christ is risen. Christ is risen. Christ is risen. Christ is risen. Christ is risen. Christ is risen. Christ is risen. Christ is risen. Christ is risen. Christ is risen. Christ is risen. Christ is risen. Christ is risen. Christ is risen. Christ is risen. Christ is risen Jesus . . .

A beat.

No! I must not! Must not! No! In Rome, here in this prison? What do I want, my God to come through the wall and rescue me? No, no!

A beat.

Christ is risen. Christ is risen Jesus show me your face again. No no no no, out of the question to pray for that! Christ is risen. Christ is risen. Christ is risen. Christ is risen. Christ is risen. Christ is risen. Christ is risen. Christ is risen. Christ is risen. Christ is risen. Christ is risen. Christ is risen. Christ is risen Jesus, oh my risen Lord, now, tonight, before I die for you, let me see your face once more . . . no, no.

A beat.

Be content with the memory. Yes. I had the revelation of my life. I saw you, thirty years ago, on the road to Damascus.

He stands, free of his chains. He turns and walks into . . .

Scene Two

*The road to Damascus, AD 34. Night beneath moon and stars.
SAUL, aged 24, is camped with BARNABAS – a captain of
the Jerusalem Temple Guards – and four of his MEN. A fire.*

SAUL. Eat, sleep. We'll wake and move on before dawn. I
want us at the city gates by sunrise.

The four GUARDS slope off, not looking at him.

(*To BARNABAS.*) What's the matter with them?

BARNABAS. They don't want to go to Damascus.

SAUL. Why not? They've arrested heretics in the past.

BARNABAS. But this time it's out of Judea.

SAUL smiles.

SAUL. When have we Jews been frightened of a raid into a
foreign country?

BARNABAS. That's not it.

SAUL. No? So what . . .

BARNABAS. The work begins to sicken them.

SAUL. But it's God's work!

BARNABAS. They're not brutes! They're Temple Guards,
simple religious men. Sometimes you're just too . . .

SAUL. Too what?

BARNABAS. Too . . . fierce.

SAUL. We are doing this to save our religion and our
country. Surely they . . .

SAUL stops, turns, as if startled by something.

BARNABAS starts, concerned.

BARNABAS. Saul?

SAUL (*sharp*). Yes?

BARNABAS. What is it?

A beat.

SAUL. Nothing. I'll speak to them.

SAUL *goes to the* GUARDS. *They are uneasy.*
BARNABAS *follows.*

Listen.

A beat.

Listen, I know how you struggle with this work. I know
how hard it is for you to arrest men and women at night,
drag them from their houses to the religious court, stand by
when they are stoned to death in the execution pits, with a
crowd screaming as if it were sport, not a terrible necessity
sanctioned by God's law. I stood by, holding men's coats.
They were stoning a young man called Stephen. With his
last breath he shouted that he would be in Paradise. His
fanaticism shocked me to the marrow of my bones. Belief
that strong could destroy the Temple itself. So I decided I
must do this thing. But I know it's not easy. It can eat into
the heart, bring bad dreams, yes?

He has touched them. They shift uneasily, hanging on every
word.

1ST GUARD. What gets to you, is the atrocities. What the
Yeshua people do. Eat the flesh . . .

2ND GUARD. Drink the blood . . .

3RD GUARD. Drink the blood, eat the flesh of helpless little
children.

1ST GUARD. You're right, Rabbi. The bad dreams are from
having to be anywhere near these people.

4TH GUARD. They're Jews like us, but what they do, it's
obscene!

BARNABAS. On the other hand, every new cult that appears is accused of eating babies.

SAUL. Yes, Barnabas. These atrocities are useful stories to the Temple, but not true. But listen, listen, we must do this work: these are dangerous times. We Jews have lived under empires over the centuries: Egypt, Babylon, Syria, Greece, now Rome . . . and we have endured. But under this occupation, under Rome, our religion itself is under attack. But where does the attack come from? Not from pagan, kiddam priests from Rome. From ourselves. Our country is torn apart by fanatics. In the cities different sects at each others throats, in the countryside whole villages gone heretical, ragged preachers on the roads with their begging bowls; Judea seethes with religious revolt. And Yeshua's not the first fanatic from Nazareth the kiddam have crucified. That particular rural slum does seem to be overrun with religious madmen.

2ND GUARD. They grow Messiahs in the fields.

3RD GUARD. The only crop: religious lunatics.

SAUL. Or it's just something in the water.

Amusement.

4TH GUARD. The back-from-the-dead magic is new, though.

2ND GUARD. Walking down off a cross? Yeah, some magic trick.

The 1ST GUARD *is not amused.*

1ST GUARD. But blasphemous. The dead will not rise.

SAUL. Oh I believe they will.

1ST GUARD. Rabbi Saul, with respect, that's because your family are Pharisees. Mine are Sadducees, for us we were made of mud and to mud we will return. The religion of Moses is for the living.

SAUL. You're wrong, you're wrong, but that doesn't divide us. Yes, we Pharisees do believe that when God ends the world, the dead will rise again. But not just one man! Who is, magically, the son of God! That is chaff, the flimflam of overheated minds. And it's not that insane doctrine that makes the Yeshua cult so dangerous to us and to our country.

1ST GUARD. The Kingdom of God is the danger.

SAUL. Yes yes, you understand: the Yeshua people call for 'the Kingdom of God'. Now. In Judea. And they find an eager audience! The people are feverish for signs and prophecies, anything to end the Roman occupation. They look for a chariot of fire to appear amongst us, they'll listen to any beautiful young man out of the desert, dressed in rags, his eyes shining with the light of a new Israel. And here we have this Yeshua sect, with its filthy blasphemy, preaching a Kingdom of God? To kiddam ears that sounds like one thing: insurrection! We must . . .

A beat. They stare at him. BARNABAS is about to move to him . . .

. . . be perfect! And the Lord God looked on Moses . . . and saw . . .

1ST GUARD. Perfect.

2ND GUARD. Saw he was perfect.

3RD GUARD. And the Lord looked on Moses and he was perfect.

SAUL. That is what we must be in this work. We must struggle to keep the religion of Moses pure. Or Judea will be drowned, not with the sea, but with Jewish blood. And that is why we are on the Damascus Road, tonight, under the stars. Be pure and we will save Judea.

They all stand.

ALL (*sing*).
Protect me, O God, in you is my refuge.
I bless Yahweh who is my counsellor,
Even at night my heart instructs me.

I keep Yahweh before me always,
For with him at my right hand, nothing can shake me.
So my heart rejoices, my soul delights,
For you will not abandon me
You will teach me the path of life,
Unbound joy in your presence,
At your right hand delight for ever.
Amen.

SAUL. Barnabas and I will take the night watch. Goodnight, God go with you.

GUARDS (*variously*). Goodnight Saul of Tarsus. / Goodnight Captain. / God go with you.

They go a distance away and prepare to sleep.

BARNABAS. Saul, I have to speak to you so don't be angry.

SAUL. Oh! I already am.

He laughs.

BARNABAS. You remember when I saw you fall? By the Temple wall?

SAUL stops laughing. They look at each other.

SAUL. Go on.

BARNABAS. Before it happened . . . there was a look about you. You . . .

SAUL is an interrupter.

SAUL. No cause to think that now. None at all. Would God let me be sick? When, come the morning, we'll be in Damascus, doing his work?

BARNABAS. Saul, you had it tonight. While you were talking to the men.

A beat.

Then SAUL smiles.

SAUL. Barnabas, you're a great worrier.

BARNABAS. Don't smarm me, what a smarmer you can be . . .

SAUL. No no, please, you're right to speak to me. I love you
for it, worry in a soldier is a great gift . . . Look, when this
thing, whatever it is, comes on me, I smell flowers.
Madness, eh?

BARNABAS. A holy madness.

SAUL. No no no no! It's a flaw. A thorn in the flesh. There's a
wrongness, cut deep inside me. God hasn't made me whole.

BARNABAS. Have you talked to the Temple priests about
this?

SAUL. Our priests are more primitive than you think, they'll
rave about casting out devils.

BARNABAS. Then consult a Greek doctor. Your family's got
the money.

SAUL *laughs.*

SAUL. Do you know what goes on in a Greek hospital?
You're given drugged wine to make you sleep. So that,
while you sleep, the god Asclepius, son of Apollo, can
appear in a dream and whisper your cure to you. There is
a limit to my love of things Greek.

BARNABAS. Do you . . .

SAUL. At this moment all I can smell is soldiers' feet and
soldiers' farts. If it does come on me, you'll know. All . . .
all that I ask is that you don't let the men see.

BARNABAS. Oh they'd love it. Prophets are meant to foam
at the mouth.

SAUL. Yes. Well, I fit that criterion.

Suddenly heated.

So many superstitions! So much to cut out of the way we
think! We are barbaric, we see only in a dark mirror, we are
all but blind to God and his world.

BARNABAS. Saul, softer. You've already preached this
evening.

SAUL. You don't think I'm a prophet, a holy man, do you,
Barnabas?

BARNABAS (*he does*). No.

SAUL. I mean, I'll roll around in the dust spitting foam if you
want.

He smiles.

BARNABAS. No.

He puts his hand on SAUL*'s arm. For a moment they are
still. Then* BARNABAS *removes his hand.*

SAUL. I'll take first watch.

BARNABAS. Are you . . .

SAUL. Wide awake!

BARNABAS. Wake me when it's my time. Don't sit through
the night on your own.

SAUL. No no. God be with you. Good night.

He moves away.

Scene Three

The GUARDS *and* BARNABAS *are asleep.*

SAUL *sits hugging his knees. He raises his head and smells
the air.*

SAUL. Jasmine?

*He is alert, looking about him. Then his head falls. He
slides onto his side, asleep.*

Out of the night a figure in a ragged loincloth comes into the camp. He has a blanket about his shoulders. It is
YESHUA.

He touches the sleeping SAUL, *whispers into his ear then steps back.*

SAUL *wakes with a start. He turns and looks at* YESHUA.

YESHUA. Saul, Saul, why do you persecute me?

SAUL. Who are you?

YESHUA. Yeshua of Nazareth, whom you want to destroy.

SAUL. No. Yeshua of Nazareth was crucified.

YESHUA. And I'm alive.

He smiles, displaying terrible wounds on his wrists. He is very relaxed, watching SAUL *with a constant gaze.*

A high-pitched noise begins, a long single note. It grows and grows until it is very loud.

Then simultaneously it stops and the stage blazes with a burst of light, which fades.

SAUL. How can that be?

YESHUA. I'm here with you.

SAUL. No one can survive a Roman crucifixion. The soldier on execution duty makes sure the criminal is dead with a wound in the side of the body . . .

YESHUA *raises his arms.* SAUL *stares at a terrible wound in* YESHUA's *side.*

YESHUA. I am with you and I am with my Father in Heaven.

SAUL. You're not real. You're a ghost! No, a demon.

YESHUA. Touch me.

SAUL. No.

YESHUA. They all want to touch me. To prove it. They stare at my wounds. The wounds are more important than anything I say. Proof? What is that? All I need to know is what my Father has told me.

SAUL. This can't be so.

YESHUA. It is so.

SAUL. No.

YESHUA. You are near to believing in it. It's in you. Growing now.

SAUL. No. What your followers say, that you came back from the dead, that can't be!

YESHUA. We are both Pharisees, Saul. We both believe in the resurrection of the dead.

SAUL. No no.

YESHUA. You long for the Kingdom of God. And it is coming. The world as you know it is about to pass away.

SAUL. No no.

YESHUA. The Kingdom of God is coming. That is why I'm with you.

SAUL. No. No no no.

YESHUA. Saul, Saul, why do you deny me, why do you kick against the truth?

SAUL *can barely stand or breathe.*

SAUL. Because!

A beat.

Because if what you say is true, you are the mystery Isaiah spoke of . . .

They quote together.

YESHUA *and* SAUL. Which for endless ages has been kept secret but will be revealed at the end of days.

SAUL. What no eye has seen and no ear has heard, what the mind of man cannot visualise.

YESHUA *and* SAUL. The secret promised by Isaiah that this age will pass away. And a new age will come.

SAUL. And God will send his son.

A silence.

Are you the Messiah, come to end the world?

A silence.

YESHUA. Is that what I am?

SAUL. I've killed your followers. If you were the Messiah you'd never have allowed their deaths.

YESHUA. The last of days is with us, they will rise from their graves in the twinkling of an eye.

SAUL. Then what? Have I been doing Satan's work? If you are what you say you are . . . it's unthinkable! How could I live with what I've done?

YESHUA. Why are you so riven inside? Why do you feel a great wrong, twisted within you? That is what you feel, isn't it?

SAUL. Yes.

A beat. He is stunned by YESHUA*'s accuracy.*

Yes. Who am I arguing with?

YESHUA. Why do you even ask?

SAUL. Am I like . . . Moses on Sinai? Challenging God?

YESHUA. My truth was always in your heart. The stronger it burnt within you, the more you fought it, the harsher you became. But now I'm with you, the struggle within you is over. This was always going to be so, Saul. Like the prophet, from when you were in your mother's womb, you were mine. But you didn't know it, and now you do.

SAUL *sinks to his knees.*

SAUL. My Lord.

YESHUA *goes to him and tries to help him to stand. But* SAUL *will not. He flinches at the sight of the nail wounds on* YESHUA'*s wrists. Then he kisses the wounds.*

YESHUA *pulls him to his feet.*

YESHUA. I'm giving you a new name. You're Saul my persecutor no longer. Now you're Paul, my follower.

PAUL. What . . . what shall I do? The guards with me . . . young killers whose minds I've . . . And the letters from the High Priest of the Temple. To the synagogues. Instructing them to give up your followers . . . I'll go back to Jerusalem. Denounce the letters! Denounce the persecution!

YESHUA. Go to Damascus. Avoid the synagogues. Find Ananias, he will help you.

PAUL. He'll think I've come to kill him.

A flicker of weariness in YESHUA. *He turns away.*

YESHUA. No, Ananias will help.

PAUL *kneels again.*

PAUL. Lord . . .

YESHUA. Go in peace, Paul.

YESHUA *kisses him on the forehead and turns to exit.*

And as PAUL *falls to the ground in a fit, the bright light dies.*

Moonlight.

Enter BARNABAS *with the* GUARDS. *They are calling out.*

BARNABAS *and* GUARDS. Saul! Saul! Saul!

1ST GUARD. There!

They find PAUL. *He is lying on his side, eyes staring.*

BARNABAS *kneels beside* PAUL.

BARNABAS. Saul! Can you hear me? Saul!

A beat.

PAUL. Who's that?

BARNABAS *turns to the* GUARDS.

BARNABAS. Go back, strike the camp, wait for us.

They hesitate.

Go!

1ST GUARD. Water.

He hands BARNABAS *a skin of water.*

BARNABAS. Thank you. Just . . . go back now.

They exit.

Saul . . .

PAUL. No one here called that.

BARNABAS. What happened?

PAUL. What happened to Saul? A mystery, a mystery.

BARNABAS. Is this your illness?

PAUL. Are you Barnabas?

BARNABAS. Yes of course.

PAUL. Barnabas, he blinded me.

BARNABAS. What do you mean? Who blinded you?

PAUL He did! The Lord!

BARNABAS. Let's get you back to the men. I'll tell them it's nothing, you're ill, you have food poisoning . . .

PAUL *laughs.*

PAUL. God's son has told me the world is about to end and
you put it down to food poisoning?

BARNABAS. Saul, please . . .

PAUL. No. I must go on to Damascus. Alone. On my knees in
the dust. In darkness. Destroyed.

BARNABAS. But the campaign, the arrests of Yeshua's
followers . . .

PAUL. Can I arrest myself? Yes, that's what I'll do. I'll crawl
in chains to Ananias to ask his forgiveness . . .

BARNABAS. You can't just abandon what we set out to do . . .

PAUL. I am fulfilling what we set out to do!

BARNABAS. You're making no sense . . .

PAUL. I saw Him. Yeshua.

A beat.

BARNABAS. Saul . . .

PAUL. Paul. Paul. That's my name now. Yeshua gave me a
new name. Say my name. If you have any love for me, any
trust in me, say my name!

BARNABAS. Stop this madness! Stop it now!

PAUL. I must be made anew. I will be. But first my name. I beg
you, say it. Paul.

BARNABAS. I won't be part of your insanity . . .

PAUL. Paul! Say it, Paul, Paul, Paul, Paul!

A beat.

BARNABAS. Paul.

PAUL, *far away, to himself.*

PAUL. No. No no no. The name means nothing. I no longer
exist. I am crossed out. Crossed out! Has He played a joke

on me? Has the shadow of the cross He died on crossed me out? That's it. That's what's been done to me.

To BARNABAS.

Help me get to Damascus.

BARNABAS.   I can't desert my post because you've had some kind of . . . fit.

PAUL.   Then I'll go alone. Give me some water.

BARNABAS.   I can't let you do this!

PAUL.   But you will.

BARNABAS.   You can't see!

PAUL.   He will lead me.

BARNABAS.   The rich man's son dabbles in religion and this is what you get! So righteous, so fanatical for the Temple, leading men into the desert then . . . all is changed!

PAUL.   You're right, it is changed.

BARNABAS.   Well, good good, how wonderful. Let's all have visions, but no! Not all of us can. You have to have money to have visions, you can't afford them on soldier's pay, they'll lose you your job. Saul, visions were for the prophets in the old times. Not us. And I must remind you that this is a military operation. We have the names of people to arrest and take back to Jerusalem for trial! This is life and death!

PAUL.   Oh yes, yes it is that . . . Barnabas, I have no strength, no mind, I'm helpless, like a newborn baby. You've believed in me. Help me.

BARNABAS *sighs. A beat, after all he has said.*

BARNABAS.   I'll send the men back to Jerusalem. I'll say . . . we've new plans . . . you and I are going to the city as spies.

PAUL.   Take me to the gates and leave me there. That's all I ask.

BARNABAS.   I can't leave you blind before a dangerous city . . .

PAUL. He will lead.

BARNABAS. 'He will lead.'

He sighs.

You sound like one of them, do you know that? A Yeshua fanatic.

PAUL. No, I'm not one of them, I'm not worthy of that.

BARNABAS *starts.*

BARNABAS. Did you hear something?

PAUL. No . . .

BARNABAS. I thought I heard someone shout.

PAUL. Shout what?

BARNABAS. Doesn't matter. Wait here. I'll go and tell the men. Water.

He gives the blind PAUL *the skin of water.*

PAUL *alone, staring out, sightless.*

In the far distance, very faintly, voices can just be heard.

VOICES. Yeshua! Yeshua! Yeshua! Yeshua!

A silence.

Lights down.

Scene Four

Arabia, AD 37. PAUL *sits before a tent. There are bundles of tent cloth – samples. He is sewing.*

There is a pile of provisions, amongst them a bucket of water, a skin of wine, bread.

An ARAB *approaches, an air of wealth and status about him.*
Two ARMED MEN *behind him keep a respectful distance.*

PAUL *stands.*

ARAB. You're the Jewish tent maker.

PAUL. Yes.

ARAB. I am Abraham, son of Feisel of Medina. I trade in
Eastern spices.

PAUL. Your good repute goes before you, Abraham, son of
Feisel. What can I offer you, bread, honey, wine . . .

ARAB. No no, not before a sale. If there is a sale. No offence.

Both are amused.

PAUL. None taken. How can I help you?

ARAB. My trade makes it necessary to go to India later in the
year. Because I can't be in my winter quarters I need a tent
that can stand rain, snow.

PAUL. I have a special cloth. Here.

PAUL *pulls out a roll of dark cloth.*

Touch.

He touches it.

ARAB. Slippery.

PAUL. The cloth is very finely woven, then rubbed with
beeswax.

ARAB. By the hands of virgins, seven times?

PAUL. If I said it were, would that increase the price you'd
pay?

ARAB. Don't you claim magic for such a cloth?

PAUL. Just skill. I can make the tent with leather flashings, to
stop water getting into the seams.

ARAB. Excellent.

PAUL. The flashings will add to the price.

ARAB. Ah we come to the price.

PAUL. The fair price.

The ARAB *laughs. They barter at great speed, trying to slap each other's hands.*

ARAB. Four Egyptian measures of gold? Or would you prefer Roman coinage?

PAUL. Gold.

ARAB. Then four . . .

PAUL. Ten.

ARAB. Five.

PAUL. Nine.

ARAB. Six.

PAUL. Seven.

ARAB. Six and a quarter.

PAUL. Six and three quarters.

ARAB. Six and a half. With the leather flashings.

A moment. Then they hit each other's hands.

PAUL. It will be ready in three weeks.

ARAB. Good good.

PAUL. Now something to eat, drink?

ARAB. Perhaps a little wine.

PAUL *pouring wine into a cup from a wineskin.*

PAUL. It's from Lebanon.

ARAB. Ah Lebanon, the cedar wood. We make boxes from it, for wealthy Roman women. To keep their love letters in. Or their poisons.

He laughs.

PAUL *offers wine.*

PAUL. For your men . . . ?

ARAB. No, they're slaves.

A beat. The ARAB *stares at* PAUL, *interested in him.*

What is your name?

PAUL. Paul.

ARAB. But that's not a Hebrew name, it's Greek.

PAUL. It was given me by my master.

ARAB. So you were a slave?

PAUL *looks at him.*

What, you ran away from your master, to hide in Arabia?

PAUL. In a manner of speaking.

The ARAB *is amused.*

ARAB. A runaway Jewish slave with a Greek name. What
strange creatures hide in our deserts. Be careful of our
demons, they can be cruel to foreigners.

PAUL. They hold no fear for me.

ARAB. Ah the Jewish God living in that huge Jerusalem
Temple. You think he will protect you against our desert
gods and goblins?

PAUL. No. But his son will.

ARAB. Son? But you Jews are 'one godders', aren't you?

PAUL. It's a mystery.

A beat.

ARAB. Forgive me, brother, let's keep our relationship strictly
commercial. I hear people get killed in Judea because of
religious arguments. All I want is a tent, not a new god.

PAUL. Thank you for your custom.

The ARAB *drains the cup and hands it back.*

ARAB. In three weeks.

PAUL *bows. The* ARAB *turns and goes, followed by his* MEN. PAUL *sits again.*

Enter BARNABAS, *a distance away.*

A silence. Then PAUL *looks up and sees him.* BARNABAS *approaches.*

PAUL. How did you find me?

BARNABAS. You thought a Jewish tent maker wouldn't be noticed in Arabia?

A beat.

Then PAUL *stands and they embrace.*

PAUL. Are you still a captain of the Temple Guard?

BARNABAS. No. I lost my enthusiasm for religious soldiering.

PAUL. Please, wine, some honey . . .

BARNABAS. Thank you.

PAUL *hands a loaf to* BARNABAS *and a wineskin. He begins to unwrap something that is wrapped in leaves.*

PAUL. Here, a honeycomb, wrapped in young date palms, they're hugely expensive. A Bedu prince gave me a whole box as a gift.

BARNABAS. You're successful.

PAUL. My father's trade. I've always loved it. So . . . What do you do now?

BARNABAS. I dig ditches.

PAUL. Yes?

BARNABAS *is amused.*

BARNABAS. That look's the rich man's son in you . . .

PAUL. No no. But you were a fine soldier.

BARNABAS. Well, now I dig irrigation ditches for vineyards. It's quite tricky.

PAUL. Yes.

BARNABAS. You're not going to ask me.

PAUL. It's for you to say.

BARNABAS. I left the Temple's service because I couldn't forget Damascus. I still can't.

A beat.

PAUL. Nor can I. Barnabas . . .

BARNABAS. I can't talk about this.

PAUL *smiles.*

PAUL. You've come all this way not to talk?

BARNABAS. It's that . . . that in Damascus I couldn't forgive myself for leaving you. Blind and raving, in a dark street, in a foreign city . . .

PAUL. And two years later here you are, come to apologise?

BARNABAS. I felt bad about it, abandoning you.

PAUL. You say 'raving'. Was I?

BARNABAS. I thought so at the time.

PAUL. And now?

A beat.

There's really no need to feel bad. You left me at the door of Ananias's house, where I'd been told to go.

BARNABAS. By Yeshua.

PAUL. By Jesus.

BARNABAS. By . . .

PAUL. His name in Latin, rather than Aramaic. It's better. Or in Greek, Christos. Christ.

BARNABAS. Christos, meaning the chosen . . .

PAUL. The Messiah. The world will understand the name 'Jesus' better, when I begin my mission.

BARNABAS. Your mission.

PAUL *smiles.*

PAUL. Now that you're here I think it's about to begin, my dear Barnabas.

BARNABAS. So Ananias . . .

PAUL. He was very frightened but he took me in.

BARNABAS. I thought he'd kill you.

PAUL. In a way, he did. He baptised me.

BARNABAS. That's one of their rites, yes?

PAUL *is sharp.*

PAUL. It's not a rite. It's something you say, I say, from my heart. You don't come to know Jesus through rites.

BARNABAS *is wrongfooted. He finds it difficult to deal with the changes in* SAUL/PAUL.

After three days my sight was restored. But they feared the Temple would send a squad from Jerusalem to find me, so they smuggled me out of the city.

Smiles.

Lowered me over the wall in a basket.

BARNABAS. They wanted to come to find you, but I talked them out of it.

PAUL. How did you do that?

BARNABAS. I told them you'd gone mad as well as blind.

PAUL *is amused.*

PAUL. Ah.

A beat.

And in Jerusalem, what of . . .

BARNABAS. Of the Yeshua people? They've gone quiet. These days they seem to have lost all their fervour. They keep themselves to themselves. It's like all these cults: the leader dies and the energy goes. A few followers keep up obscure rituals in secret, then it all fades away. Our campaign to persecute them was probably pointless. Now they lock their doors and worship their Yeshua or whatever you want to call Him.

PAUL. Why are you so bitter?

BARNABAS. I . . .

PAUL. You want to believe in Him.

BARNABAS *cannot reply.*

It's growing in your soul . . .

BARNABAS. Oh this Pharisee talk of the soul . . .

PAUL. You can feel it. You can hardly breathe because of it.

BARNABAS. It's that . . . if a man like you can be so changed by a dead man . . .

PAUL. He's not dead, Barnabas! Not dead.

BARNABAS. I can't accept I . . .

PAUL. He said to me: 'Why do you kick against the truth?'

BARNABAS. No.

PAUL. He's saying it to you. You can hear Him.

BARNABAS. No.

PAUL. Barnabas, why do you kick against the truth?

BARNABAS. Perhaps . . . if you baptised me . . . I'd believe in Him.

PAUL *is being very gentle.*

PAUL. No no no no, my dear friend. Wrong way round. Faith is first.

BARNABAS. But everyone in the Yeshua community is baptised.

PAUL. Oh yes.

BARNABAS. But I can't get baptised unless I have faith.

PAUL. It would be meaningless.

BARNABAS. So how do I get 'faith'? What is it? A feeling? A fever? A what?

PAUL. Can you say this? 'I believe Christ died for our sins. He was buried. On the third day He was raised to life.'

BARNABAS. 'I believe Christ died for our sins He was buried on the third day . . . '

PAUL. No no no no no! You're just mouthing, not believing, like a merchant chanting in a temple of Apollo hoping for good trade, like a girl kneeling before Diana wanting a husband. You can't buy faith!

BARNABAS. I don't understand!

PAUL. You do!

BARNABAS. Just throw the water over me and say the words!

PAUL. Don't do this lightly. Do this lightly and God will condemn you, along with all of the unbelieving world.

A beat.

Is He in your heart?

BARNBABAS. Yes. I think. Yes! Why do you think I'm here?

A beat.

PAUL. Kneel down.

He picks up a bucket of water.

Say: 'Christ is Lord.'

BARNABAS. Are you going to throw that over me?

PAUL. If there was a river I'd throw you in it. So I'm making do.

Amusement. BARNABAS *kneels.*

BARNABAS. 'Christ is Lord.'

PAUL. Say: 'I belong to Christ.'

BARNABAS. 'I belong to Christ.'

PAUL. Then I baptise you in the name of Jesus.

He pours the bucket of water over BARNABAS. *He splutters, he laughs.*

PAUL *grasps* BARNABAS*'s hands and pulls him up.*

There is a ritual.

BARNABAS. I knew it!

PAUL. No, it's nothing like a Roman ritual or a ritual of the Temple. It gains you nothing. It's in memory of Jesus. Ananias taught it to me in Damascus.

He lifts the half-eaten loaf of bread.

On the night that Jesus was betrayed He was with His followers. They were having a meal. He took some bread, gave thanks and divided it.

PAUL *pulls some of the bread from the loaf.*

He said, 'Eat this, this is my body, which is for you, do this in memory of me.'

He hands the piece of bread to BARNABAS. *He eats it, slowly.* PAUL *takes a piece and eats it.*

PAUL *lifts the wineskin.*

And after the meal He lifted a cup of wine and said, 'This is the new covenant in my blood. Drink it in memory of me.'

He hands BARNABAS *the wineskin, he drinks from it. Then* PAUL *drinks from it.*

They look at each other.

BARNABAS. Bread and wine. That's where the baby-eating, blood-drinking stories come from.

PAUL. Yes.

BARNABAS. What . . .

Tries to laugh.

What do I do now?

PAUL. Go back to Jerusalem with me. I must see Jesus's brother. I'll finish the jobs I've got and we'll go. No time to lose! It's been revealed to me, you see. The Kingdom of God Jesus preached? It's coming.

BARNABAS. 'The Kingdom of God' – that's what we were trying to stop!

PAUL. But now I know what it means. Barnabas, Jesus is coming back to us, any day, any moment. The Kingdom of God doesn't mean a revolt against the Romans. It means the end of the world.

PAUL *leaves the scene and returns to the prison.*

Scene Five

Rome, AD 65. Prison.

PAUL. The questions, who was that? Young woman. Clever.
From Corinth. So much trouble in Corinth, three visits. The
letters. Yes, she said: 'If the world is about to end, why are
people dying amongst us?' Answer? Easy. They will rise
with Him. On the last day. Which can come . . . now. Before
I . . . before I clap my hands!

A beat.

*He claps his hands. He waits. He claps them again. He
waits. He claps his hands. Then he falls to his knees and
prays.*

Dear Lord, your servant waits.

The loud noise of a heavy door opening.

Two GAOLERS *drag* PETER *in. He struggles.* PETER *is a
big man. They wrestle him down to the ground and fix
chains on his legs.*

PETER *shouts at them. Accent: he is not an educated man.*

PETER. Get off me, I'm not fighting you . . . get off me,
Kiddam bastards!

1ST GAOLER. What? What are we?

Kicks PETER. *He howls.*

What are we?

2ND GAOLER. Christian filth . . .

1ST GAOLER, *kicking him again.*

1ST GAOLER. What are we, baby killer?

PETER. You are lost sheep. With shit hanging out your arses!

2ND GAOLER. What? What did you say?

PAUL. For mercy's sake leave him alone!

1ST GAOLER. Oh mercy mercy's sake . . .

He kicks PAUL.

The CHIEF GAOLER *steps out of the darkness. He carries linen cloth and a wooden bucket of water.*

CHIEF GAOLER. All right, let 'em alone! They could have a visit tonight. From a very distinguished person. Don't want them to stand there with faces like cabbages.

PETER. What visitor?

CHIEF GAOLER. Well, you'll just have to shit yourselves waiting to see, won't you.

PAUL. The only visit we crave is by the Risen Lord.

2ND GAOLER. Oh gobbyledegook, shut your mouth . . .

The 2ND GUARD *about to kick* PAUL.

CHIEF GAOLER. No no . . .

PETER. Who will visit? A magistrate? To reopen our cases? Release us?

CHIEF GAOLER. I tell you your only hope of release is if your God magics a hole in that wall, magics your chains away and magics you out of here in a cloud.

PAUL. What do you believe in?

The GAOLER *is startled by the question.*

CHIEF GAOLER. I believe in a mystery, baby killer. In a secret place. A holy cave, where you can never go.

The CHIEF GOALER *signals to the other two* GAOLERS *and turns to go.*

PAUL. So you believe in the Lord of Light.

The CHIEF GAOLER *stops in his tracks.*

The Victorious One. The Warrior. The God of Truth. The Giver of Bliss. The Saviour from Death. Mithras.

The CHIEF GAOLER *turns.*

We are both religious men.

CHIEF GAOLER. Don't you dare to compare the obscene teachings of your crucified criminal, with the glory of the Lord Mithras.

PAUL. I don't compare them. But the followers of Jesus and the followers of Mithras long for the same thing.

CHIEF GAOLER. I swear I'll have you lashed through your ribs to your lungs, Christian. When you reach the execution ground you'll be a sack of blood.

PETER *(low).* Paul, the man's a brute . . .

But PAUL *is calm, and persists.*

PAUL. You and I, we believe in the immortality of the soul.

The CHIEF GAOLER *is taken aback.*

You and I, we believe life has triumphed over death. Mithras killed a bull in a cave. That's how you think he overcame death.

CHIEF GAOLER. I can't talk about these mysteries, baby killer . . .

PAUL. The Lord Jesus came back from the dead. He is alive, now, He's not a painting on the end wall of a Mithras lodge, He's a living being. He wants to come to you, and to be in your heart, and save you when the end of the world comes. Imagine the glory when He calls the dead from their graves. And He leads those who followed Him, the dead and the living, to Heaven. You could be one of them.

A beat.

CHIEF GAOLER. Yeah, well, pretty picture.

PAUL. No, it will happen soon! The end of the world! In our lifetime! Tonight! Or, now, right now, it could be a moment away!

He claps his hands.

A moment of unease from the CHIEF GAOLER *then he laughs.*

CHIEF GAOLER. Your executions are set. Come the morning, you're for the banks of death's river, or wherever you Jews have your hell. Here's some water, some cloth, clean yourselves up. And . . . no singing. Or I'll have your faces kicked in after all.

Nods to the other GAOLERS.

I can't stand Christian hymns. They make my teeth go funny.

The GAOLERS *exit.*

PAUL, *chains dragging, goes to* PETER.

PAUL. Peter.

They embrace.

The peace of Jesus be with you.

PETER. And with you.

PAUL. When did they arrest you?

PETER. Two weeks ago. With ten others. The congregation is terrified.

PAUL. I thought after they'd taken me, they'd leave the congregation alone.

PETER. Your sense of your own importance hasn't exactly taken a knock.

PAUL. I only hoped for peace. And that the Lord would come.

PETER. Ah the end of days, yes. Well. If it comes before the morning it'll spare us a certain amount of dis . . . discomfort.

He cannot stop his hand trembling.

PAUL. Peter, my brother . . .

PETER. No, I'm all right. At the moment. Who knows what state I'll be in come sunrise . . .

PAUL. A state of grace.

PETER. Yes. Yes, well.

A beat.

We couldn't reach you in prison, we tried.

PAUL. They kept me in solitary confinement.

PETER. When did they condemn you?

PAUL. A month ago.

PETER. We watched the magistrates' courts, we never saw you brought to trial.

PAUL. I appeared before the Emperor's court.

PETER. The Emperor's court . . .

PAUL. I'm a citizen of the Roman Empire, remember? The legal niceties must be seen to be kept.

PETER. Was the Emperor himself there?

PAUL. Oh yes.

PETER. Did you speak to him?

PAUL. I told him I wanted to die on the cross, like my Saviour.

PETER. What did he say?

PAUL. Nothing. He was wearing a mask with a woman's face.

PETER. In Heaven's name, Paul, you can have the axe, as a Roman citizen that's your right . . .

PAUL. No no, the axe it will be. They couldn't have a Roman citizen die a non-citizen's death.

PETER. Where will they take us?

PAUL. The execution ground at the third milepost on the Appian way.

PETER. After all these years it comes to this.

PAUL. Tomorrow we'll be in Paradise.

PETER. After all these years, to die in Rome, not Jerusalem.

PAUL. It's His will.

PETER. Oh yes, His will.

PAUL. Peter?

PETER. Never your will, was it, Paul?

PAUL. What's the matter?

PETER *is overcome with fury.*

PETER. Matter? What's the matter? It's because of you we're dying in Rome. The mission to the Gentiles? Congregations in Corinth, Athens, Ephesus, even here in Rome? All this was never meant to be!

PAUL *is shocked.*

PAUL. The mission to the Gentiles was ordered by Christ.

PETER. Yeshua never preached that.

PAUL. That is a terrible thing to say!

PETER. The mission to the Gentiles came from you.

PAUL. Peter, I know why you're talking like this, but we mustn't be afraid, He Himself must have felt terrible fear . . .

PETER. No no, you don't understand! You can't understand! My life is a lie!

PAUL. I beg you, stop this. We're not the only people to die for His truth.

PETER *is near to weeping.*

PETER. His truth, His truth, His truth.

A beat.

No I . . . forgive me. But when you saw Him on the way to Damascus, He never told you to travel endlessly around the world converting kiddam and pagans. Did He?

PAUL. He told me in my heart, when I was in Arabia. Through my faith. What I felt in the heart.

PETER. I always thought that bit of your teaching was dangerous. Terrible sins can flow from what you feel in the heart.

PAUL. I had it from the Lord that I was right. In the Jerusalem Temple, when I was praying and fell into a trance.

PETER. Yes. Your trance in the Temple.

PAUL. I fell into a trance and He told me to leave Jerusalem.

PETER. Paul, it was in James's house.

PAUL. He sent me out into the world with his blessing.

PETER. You saw him when you came to James's house, with Barnabas.

PAUL. No, it was in the Temple, He appeared to me in the Temple . . .

PETER. No, you don't remember properly. You had an attack . . .

PAUL. It was in the Temple!

PETER. I know it was in James's house, Paul.

PAUL, *remembering.*

PAUL. James's house, in Jerusalem . . .

Scene Six

Jerusalem, AD 37. The house of JAMES, YESHUA*'s brother.* PAUL *and* BARNABAS.

BARNABAS. I can't face them.

PAUL. They'll understand.

BARNABAS. I can't. I don't want them to know who I am, what I did.

PAUL. I did worse, I led the persecution. Face them. These are wise and good men.

BARNABAS. Jesus's brother, no, I can't.

PAUL. Then wait for me in the street.

BARNABAS. No, I should stay, what if they become violent . . .

PAUL smiles.

PAUL. They won't harm me. The Lord Jesus will speak to their hearts. Go.

BARNABAS, unhappy, exits.

A beat.

MARY MAGDALENE enters. She is 25 years old. Accent: uneducated.

PAUL. Lady . . .

MARY. You're Saul of Tarsus.

PAUL. I've a new name.

MARY. Yes, Yeshua gave it to you.

PAUL. You know . . .

MARY. Know your story? Oh yeah. They're arguing about whether to meet you or not.

PAUL. Can I ask your name?

MARY. I'm Mary. Yeshua's wife.

A beat.

He kneels.

What you doing . . .

PAUL. It's a blessing to meet you.

MARY. Get up!

PAUL. I thank God for the privilege . . .

MARY. No no, don't do that. I'm sick of religious men
kneeling in front of me. They usually want to wash my feet.

PAUL *stands.*

PAUL. Forgive me I . . .

MARY. Yeshua was kneeling in front of me when he asked me
to marry him. Washing my feet. I told him when we were
hitched that would stop.

PAUL. It's that I didn't know He married.

MARY. His brother keeps it very quiet.

PAUL. Do you still see your husband? Does He appear to
you?

MARY *laughs.*

MARY. You really are one of 'em, aren't you? The 'God's
sonners'.

PAUL. The . . .

MARY. The lunatics who say Yeshua was God's son.

PAUL. You of all people must know that He was.

MARY. Oh really? You think bed with him was some kind of
mystical experience?

PAUL. I . . .

MARY. Know why he married me? To spite his mother and
father. They're rich, you know. Own just about the only
business in Nazareth, employ half the village. Wood
workshops. They're stuck up too: aristocratic blood, 'We are
of the House of David' blah blah, they love all that. They
saw Yeshua as High Priest one day, paid through the nose
for him to be taught at the Temple in Jerusalem. Bright little
kid he was too, they say. Knew the Torah off by heart. So

when Yeshua took to the road with no shoes and a begging bowl, they weren't well pleased. Nothing compared though, to when he married me. They didn't like that, not one bit. But he was over thirty so he could insist. His mother was in charge of the wedding party of course, so you know what she did? Served water. Yeshua had wine brought in. No, they didn't it like one bit, having a daughter-in-law who was a whore.

A beat.

PAUL *is bewildered.*

PAUL. He married you to save you?

MARY. Yeah, he saved me. If he hadn't taken a liking to me, I'd be dead by now. Or good as, lying in a gutter outside a Roman barracks.

Looks around nervously.

I've got to go, they mustn't find me here.

PAUL. One thing, lady, please . . . Were you there when He died?

She stares at him, shocked.

Forgive me, it must be painful for you, but we who weren't there, we long for the words, the look, the . . . touch of the real Christ.

MARY. Christ?

PAUL. Yeshua. You were there? As His wife?

MARY. I can't talk about this.

He grabs her wrist.

PAUL. You saw Him buried. You went to the burial ground.

MARY. Yeah all right, I went there. With his mother. Three days later . . .

PAUL. Three days. He rose in three days?

MARY. I can't talk about this.

PAUL. You were a witness, you were there, I must have the authentic . . .

MARY. All right!

She pulls her arm away.

Sometimes I think men want religion more than they want sex.

PAUL. What did you see?

MARY. There was nothing to see.

PAUL. The grave . . .

MARY. It was a tomb, some rich friend had paid.

PAUL. He was in the tomb.

MARY. I can't talk about this.

PAUL. He wasn't.

MARY. No.

PAUL. His body wasn't in the tomb.

MARY. It's a secret.

PAUL. The tomb was empty.

MARY. I said it's a secret.

PAUL. But you want to tell me.

MARY. It's too terrible. What it means, it's . . . too terrible to say.

PAUL. The tomb was empty.

A beat.

MARY, *a whisper.*

MARY. Yes.

PAUL. Did you see any one?

MARY. There was a bit of garden there, and a man.

PAUL. A gardener?

MARY. A man.

PAUL. Did he say anything to you?

MARY. He said Yeshua wasn't there.

PAUL. And?

MARY. Nothing else, he went away . . .

PAUL. Was it Him? Was it Yeshua?

MARY. No! No . . .

PAUL. Maybe He looked different, transformed, after He had risen . . .

MARY. No, nothing like that! It wasn't him! No.

She turns to go.

PAUL. Tell me just one thing, I beg you. Since the garden, have you seen Him?

She looks at him.

MARY. I don't want to be a holy woman. I don't want men on their knees praying to me, I don't want my fucking feet washed any more.

She runs away and exits.

A moment.

Then JAMES, *aged 28, and* PETER, *aged 35, enter.* JAMES *is aggressive.*

JAMES. Have you got men waiting in the street?

PAUL. No . . .

JAMES. Soldiers, waiting for a signal?

PAUL. No . . .

JAMES. That thug you came with, has he sneaked away to tell them the layout of the house? So he can lead them in here and arrest us all?

PAUL. No, send someone to look!

JAMES. Oh we have.

PAUL. Then you know I'm alone.

JAMES *looks at* PAUL.

A beat.

JAMES. All I know about you is that you had forty-two of us stoned to death, fifteen of them women. Then, mercifully, you disappeared. Now after three years, suddenly here you are, in Jerusalem, with a new name. You must expect a certain . . . reserve from us. Suspicion. Loathing. Dread.

PAUL. With my head bowed, weighted down by your anger, in sorrow and shame, in the deepest remorse, before God I beg your forgiveness for what I did in my old life.

JAMES. Oh your 'old life', you have a new one now?

PAUL. I lived within Judaism, there was simply no limit to the way I persecuted you. In my attempts to destroy, I know I outstripped all my contemporaries in my limitless enthusiasm for the traditions of our ancestors. But God had set me apart from the time I was in my mother's womb. And has called me to reveal His son to the world.

JAMES. You really want us to believe that someone could change so much?

PAUL. Nothing prepared me for the revelation. There is no human explanation for it. I hid myself away, I couldn't come to you. I waited for His truth to work in me.

PETER *is moved by this. He is about to speak but* JAMES *makes a sign to him to keep silent.*

JAMES. And now 'truth' has 'worked' inside you, you've decided to present yourself.

PAUL. You are the Lord's brother, James?

JAMES *sighs.*

JAMES. Yes.

PAUL *kneels.*

JAMES *turns away.*

PAUL. Give me your blessing.

JAMES. Yes. Yes, you have my blessing. Now get up.

PAUL. Your blessing in the name of the risen Lord.

JAMES *and* PETER *glance at each other.*

JAMES. You have it.

PAUL *stands, looking from* JAMES *to* PETER.

PAUL. May I meet the other apostles?

JAMES. I think not.

PAUL. I would like to draw spiritual strength from them . . .

JAMES. If you want spiritual strength, live according to
       Yeshua's teachings. I give thanks for your change of heart.
       But as leader of the congregation here, I have to tell you:
       leave Jerusalem, go back to wherever you came from.

PAUL. You don't understand. He has asked me to be His
       messenger.

JAMES. He?

PAUL. The Lord. He has made me an apostle.

JAMES. Only the Jerusalem congregation can appoint
       apostles.

PAUL. Though on the Lord's authority.

JAMES *irritated.*

JAMES. You keep on calling him the . . .

Controls his temper.

Let me be clear to you. The authority amongst Yeshua's
followers lies with his family and those who knew him
when he was teaching.

PAUL. Of course I want your authority for my mission.

JAMES. Mission.

PAUL. To take the Gospel to the world.

JAMES. 'Gospel', what is this Greek word?

PAUL. Euangelion. The good news. That the Lord is risen.
And is coming again. That we are in the last days and any
time, any day, night, the Kingdom Of God will come. As
Yeshua preached.

JAMES *sighs.*

JAMES. My brother did preach the coming of the Kingdom of
God. But in a religious sense. He didn't mean the overthrow
of Rome in Judea and he didn't mean what you seem to
think: Armageddon. The end of the world.

PAUL. But He did. That's why He died on the cross and rose
again, to show that in Him, we will all be brought to life,
the living and the dead. Jew and Gentile.

JAMES. I am telling you he did not teach that! My brother's
message was for Jews.

PAUL. What then did he mean by the 'Kingdom of God'?

JAMES. It is something in the hearts of devout people.

PAUL. But, you say, just for Jews?

JAMES. Yeshua wanted to cleanse the Temple, not pull it
down! To purify Judaism, not deny it. The last three years
we have worked to make the authorities, the kiddam and the
Temple priests, understand that. The teaching of Yeshua is
no threat. He was a great religious reformer.

PAUL. 'Reformer'? He came to change everything, to end
everything, not 'reform' it!

JAMES. Do not tell me what my brother did or did not preach! I was with him. You weren't.

PAUL. But I have seen Him. He has called me.

JAMES. Yes, your so-called 'conversion' was reported to us from Damascus.

PAUL. 'So-called'?

A beat.

Why can't we understand each other? Why aren't we at one in His name?

JAMES. Fear of false teaching.

PAUL. Not from me.

JAMES. No?

A beat.

PAUL. Do you believe He is the Son of God?

JAMES. That is . . . beyond me.

PAUL. Do you believe he is the Messiah? You must, you're His brother . . .

JAMES. That is . . . a mystery.

PAUL. Do you believe He rose from the dead to bring us eternal life?

JAMES. How dare you attempt to put me through some kind of crackpot catechism!

PAUL. 'Crackpot'? But you let your followers believe He rose from the dead. The Damascus congregation, they believe it. And you don't stop them! Ananias baptised me into a new life and the world to come! Did that mean nothing?

JAMES. Ananias baptised you.

PAUL. Yes.

JAMES. He had no authority from us to do that.

PAUL. The only authority is with the Lord.

JAMES. But through us in Jerusalem. We are the family, the first followers, we are the tradition!

PAUL. Of course I hold you in great esteem. I know I stand before true apostles. But I have to say this: the Gospel I am to preach is from me, told to me. I have not received it from any human being, I was not taught it, it came to me from a revelation on the road to Damascus. Direct from Jesus Christ.

JAMES. Jesus, Christ, Christos . . . What? Are we now to latinise and greekify my brother's name?

PAUL. If His Gospel is to be understood by Gentiles: yes!

PETER. You want to preach to pagans, not to Jews? That's what you're saying?

PAUL *looks at* PETER *for the first time.*

PAUL. Forgive me . . .

PETER. I'm Cephas.

PAUL. Cephas. The man He called Peter, the fisherman?

PETER. You heard bad things of me?

PAUL. No, no, only good, in Damascus they said you were the first to join Him. The Lord depended upon you.

PETER. Did they tell you He called me His 'rock'?

PAUL. Yes.

PETER. I wasn't.

JAMES. Peter . . .

PETER. So you want to preach outside Judea?

PAUL. Yes. Take the Gospel to cities, ports, Roman and Greek, throughout the pagan world.

PETER. And you're talking about what, starting new congregations, amongst Jews abroad?

PAUL. No no, I said, to the Gentiles!

PETER. So what, you'll circumcise Romans, Greeks, Arabs, Africans?

PAUL. It doesn't matter if they're circumcised or not.

PETER. But they must be converted to Judaism. If they're to follow Yeshua.

JAMES. That's right. Yeshua spoke only to the Jews, for the Jews.

And PAUL *snaps inside.*

PAUL. Stupidity! Stupidity! Three years and what has happened? You're behind locked doors, fearful, looking inward. In guarding a great truth you are letting it wither! The world is waiting, in darkness, for the good news of its Saviour.

PETER. Delivered by you, eh? Not by the people who loved Him, and suffered with Him and . . .

JAMES. Peter, no. We must talk. (*To* PAUL.) Forgive us. We who knew him and were with him at the end, we bear a heavy responsibility.

PAUL. Of course.

They go.

PAUL *kneels and prays.*

Jesus, hope of the world. I prayed so hard in the Temple before coming here. So hard I . . . almost saw you again. Tell me, am I right? Am I your apostle? Do I hear you?

He stops. YESHUA, *ill, wrapped in blankets, shuffles through a side door into the room. He stands looking at* PAUL.

YESHUA. Paul.

PAUL *turns. There is a silence. Then he kneels.*

PAUL. My Lord.

YESHUA. Paul, leave Jerusalem.

PAUL. Yes! To do your work . . .

YESHUA. There are people here who want to kill you. They won't accept you.

PAUL. So it is your will.

YESHUA. Leave Jerusalem.

PAUL. I thought first to Syria . . .

YESHUA. Yes yes, but go.

PAUL. To preach your Gospel to the pagans.

YESHUA *is distressed.*

YESHUA. What have I done to you?

PAUL. You've given me life.

PAUL *reaches out to him.*

YESHUA *holds out a hand in a blessing.*

The high-pitched noise, a single note, heard in the Damascus road scene, begins again. It becomes very loud.

PAUL *falls to the stage. As he does so, the lights go to blackout and the noise stops.*

MARY. He's fainted.

JAMES. Paul, Paul!

MARY. How long has he been lying there . . . ?

JAMES. Paul!

Lights up.

PAUL *is coming to.* JAMES *and* MARY *are helping him to his feet.* YESHUA *is not there.*

Do you want to lie down or . . .

PAUL. No no. No.

JAMES. Some water . . .

PAUL. No no. Listen! The Lord has told me to do this work.

JAMES*'s manner has changed. He treats* PAUL
condescendingly, as if he is talking to a madman – which
JAMES *thinks he is.*

JAMES. I know he has. And we will help you.

PAUL. Yes?

JAMES. Are you sure you don't want to rest . . .

PAUL. No, this is nothing. You will help me?

JAMES. You can preach your Gospel, your . . . good news . . .
to the pagans. With our authority.

PAUL. The Lord has told me to go first to Syria, then to
Galatia.

JAMES. Good.

PAUL. I give thanks that the Lord has changed your hearts.

PETER. Paul, you can stay at my house, while you prepare.
For a week or two.

PAUL. Yes! You can tell me all you know about Him . . .

JAMES. But there is one condition.

PAUL. Yes yes, what . . .

JAMES. When you are on your 'preaching tours' . . .

PAUL. My ministry . . .

JAMES. . . . . You collect money for us. Our people are poor.

A beat.

PAUL. Money? Yes. God loves a cheerful giver. Proverbs.

JAMES. To the needy he gave without stint, his uprightness stands firm forever. Ps . . .

PAUL. . . . Psalms.

JAMES. Yes.

PAUL. I will now take the gospel of the living Jesus to the world.

Interval.

Scene Seven

Rome, AD 65. Prison. PAUL *and* PETER.

PETER. Paul . . . have you ever thought that you may be wrong?

PAUL *is surprised. He has never thought such a thing.*

PAUL. Wrong?

A beat.

About what?

PETER. About all you have done.

PAUL. Oh many, many times! I was wrong to fall out with Barnabas, that time in Corinth. I should never have let that happen. I should have convinced him I was right.

PETER. So you were wrong because you didn't convince him you were right.

PAUL. I was deeply at fault.

PETER. But not wrong.

PAUL. Peter, what are you trying to . . .

PETER. Have you never had a flicker of doubt?

PAUL. Of my suitability of course, none of us are worthy to . . .

PETER. No no, I mean . . . flicker of doubt about the truth.

PAUL. You mean in the Hebrew sense? Truth meaning reliability, firmness? Oh many, many times, I've felt weak, uncertain what to do, incapable . . .

PETER. No no, Paul! How can I possibly explain to you . . .

PAUL. Oh you mean 'truth' in the Greek sense. Yes of course. The appearance of the world hides, smears, darkens the reality of Christ's message. But we will see truth face to face, Jesus face to face. I will know Him as certainly as I know myself.

PETER. What if you are wrong? The mission is wrong, what you and I have given our lives to is wrong?

A beat.

PAUL. The truth has been revealed to us.

PETER. So what you know you know!

PAUL. The truth we preach can't be wrong. It's as it is in Jesus.

PETER. You tangle things up, so tightly!

PETER *turns away, despairing.*

PAUL. Peter, Peter, I nearly despaired in Corinth. The congregation were at each other's throats. All the old problems were tearing us apart. And I thought, has Christ left me?

BARNABAS *enters for the next scene.* PAUL *stands and walks into it.*

Scene Eight

Corinth, AD 56. BARNABAS *and* PAUL. BARNABAS *has a letter.*

BARNABAS. James writes asking about when you will bring the money to Jerusalem.

PAUL *is tired and bad tempered.*

PAUL. Always the money. Are the leaders of the congregation here?

BARNABAS. Waiting for you.

PAUL. What's their mood?

BARNABAS. Ugly. They're split into factions, arguing all the time.

PAUL. Over what?

BARNABAS. The usual. Meat-eating and sex.

PAUL. And are there babblers?

BARNABAS. Yes, they speak in tongues.

PAUL *is irritated.*

PAUL. Why must they do that? It's breaking out in every congregation.

BARNABAS. If you preach that the Spirit moves, they'll babble.

PAUL. Yes but in moderation! Not for hours writhing on the floor. What else does James say?

BARNABAS. He asks if you are still baptising men who haven't been circumcised.

PAUL. He's not still going on about who's gashed and who's not?

BARNABAS. He's concerned that if Gentiles are not circumcised, baptism means nothing.

PAUL. Write back that I am laying down a clear rule for the congregations. If a man who is called is circumcised, obviously he stays as he is. When an uncircumcised man is called, let him stay as he is. It doesn't matter! If a slave is called to Christ, he is a freeman of the Lord. In the same way a free man who is called is a slave of Christ. Please, please can we stop arguing about this! Building a congregation is not a matter of piling up foreskins!

BARNABAS. James's point is that if they are not circumcised they can never convert to Judaism. And I agree with him.

A beat.

PAUL. You what?

BARNABAS. Paul, I'm going back to Cyprus.

PAUL. You can't. When we've finished here we're going to Ephesus.

BARNABAS. I'm telling you that I'm leaving your mission.

PAUL. Why? Because we disagree about foreskins?

BARNABAS. I'm worn out. Tired men long to return to what they once were, Paul. And I was a conservative Jew, working for the Temple. You've invented too many new teachings.

PAUL. I have invented nothing! I pass on what I have received from the Lord.

BARNABAS. I'm going to Cyprus to rest.

PAUL. We can't rest.

BARNABAS. You wear out the people around you. Or fall out with them. Apollos isn't in Corinth anymore, why?

PAUL. Apollos was beginning to preach Greek philosophy that has nothing to do with the Lord's message. No matter. The Lord brings me helpers.

BARNABAS. And you exhaust them.

PAUL. I must minister to the leaders of the congregation, they're waiting.

BARNABAS. Oh yes, minister to them, the 'flock', but not to us, your helpers.

PAUL. We must be selfless in this work.

BARNABAS. Is that how you see yourself? As selfless?

PAUL. Others cannot be as I am, I know.

BARNABAS. No, they cannot. They want families. Comfort. At times to get drunk. To be confused. To be less than perfect. To have sex for pleasure. Pleasure, Paul! To have something else on their minds other than the end of the world!

PAUL. It is hard not to think of the end of the world. Why Cyprus?

BARNABAS. I need a holiday. And John Luke is there.

BARNABAS *turns away.*

PAUL. You're going now? This moment?

BARNABAS. It's best.

PAUL. Stay for the meeting.

BARNABAS. No. I've heard you preach, many times, Paul.

PAUL *sweet-talks.*

PAUL. I know I know, I'm not the greatest speaker. No eloquence, not like Apollos with his flowery, clever-clever rhetoric. Twirly Greek mannerisms? I'll reconcile with him, you're right about that. It was wrong, I was short-tempered.

He smiles.

Tired.

BARNABAS. You won't talk me round.

PAUL. I have something new to say, I'd like you to hear it. Very well: desert me. Desert the work. Have your holiday.

He turns away. BARNABAS *is shocked by the abruptness.*

BARNABAS. I'll stay, to sing the hymn.

PAUL. As you wish.

He walks into the meeting room. The LEADERS OF THE CONGREGATION *at Corinth are played by members of the cast.* PAUL *is in the crossfire of their questions. There is no trace of his bad temper.*

BARNABAS *stands a distance away, watching* PAUL.

Grace to you, brothers of Corinth, and peace from God our Father and the Lord Jesus Christ.

CORINTHIANS. Grace to you, Paul.

PAUL. Now. What is this about meat?

1ST CORINTHIAN. It's when we eat with pagans.

2ND CORINTHIAN. The meat . . .

3RD CORINTHIAN. If the meat is from a sacrifice to a pagan god . . . should we eat it?

4TH CORINTHIAN. Meat from pagan sacrifice is defiled!

2ND CORINTHIAN. But most of the cooked meat in the shops is from sacrifices.

5TH CORINTHIAN. Revolting!

PAUL. Listen, listen to me. Eat anything from the butchers, it doesn't matter. Psalms: 'To the Lord belongs the earth and all it contains.' And if you're eating with pagans, eat what they eat, what does it matter? On the other hand if you're with someone who is revolted by this . . . don't eat it. What does that matter? Simply respect the conscience of others. Don't be a cause of offence to Jews or Greeks, believers or pagans.

2ND CORINTHIAN. If a member of the congregation steals from me, should I take him to the pagan courts?

3RD CORINTHIAN. Yes, if one of us steals from another.

5TH CORINTHIAN. Or defrauds them.

PAUL. This has happened?

A beat.

4TH CORINTHIAN. Yes.

2ND CORINTHIAN. Yes.

PAUL. Then you should be ashamed.

3RD CORINTHIAN. But I want justice.

PAUL. It's shameful. Unbelievers must not see us prosecuting each other in the courts whatever the crime.

3RD CORINTHIAN. But I was swindled, by a man who called himself my brother in Christ . . .

PAUL. Then prefer to be swindled. Do you not realise that people who do evil will never inherit the Kingdom of God? Make no mistake – the sexually immoral, idolaters, adulterers, the self-indulgent, sodomites, thieves, misers, drunkards, slanderers and swindlers, none of these will inherit the Kingdom of God.

1ST CORINTHIAN. You're harsh.

5TH CORINTHIAN. Sexual morality, here it comes.

4TH CORINTHIAN. Paul. Immorality is rife amongst us.

5TH CORINTHIAN. There is nothing immoral about the human body!

1ST CORINTHIAN. Yes and Christ has made us free. So everything is permissible.

Agreement and disagreement.

PAUL. Maybe it is, but not everything does good. True, for me everything is permissible, but I am determined not to be dominated by anything. Keep away from sexual immorality.

2ND CORINTHIAN. Why so strong on that, Paul?

5TH CORINTHIAN. Always down on sex.

Amusement.

PAUL. Keep away from it because all other sins that someone may commit are done outside the body. But the sexually immoral person sins against his own body.

5TH CORINTHIAN. But our bodies belong to us.

PAUL. No, they do not. You are not your own property, you have been bought at a price. Don't you realise that your bodies are members of Christ's body? Do you think you can take parts of Christ's body and join them to the body of a prostitute? Out of the question! So use your body for the glory of God.

1ST CORINTHIAN. That's fine for you.

2ND CORINTHIAN. You're a celibate.

3RD CORINTHIAN. You think it's a good thing for a man not to touch a woman at all.

PAUL. Yes, to the unmarried and the widowers amongst you I'd say: it's good for them to stay as they are, like me.

He smiles.

But if you must, better to marry than to burn.

Amusement.

Don't torment yourselves, be free from worry about these matters. Think of what's to come. Time is short. The world as we know it is passing away.

2ND CORINTHIAN. The world as we know it is passing away. Albra, casawa, iluthia halawah, locai!

4TH CORINTHIAN. Locai yereaway, hathacarata!

CORINTHIANS. Amen! Amen!

PAUL. Yes, speak in tongues but interpret.

3RD CORINTHIAN. Telark, forad, nanianth, heggar calish!

PAUL. Yes, brother, be moved by the Spirit but know what the Spirit is telling you.

1ST CORINTHIAN. We must all speak in tongues!

5TH CORINTHIAN. All must be prophets!

3RD CORINTHIAN. The Spirit is here! Now!

4TH CORINTHIAN. The language of angels!

CORINTHIANS. Garak fetidit, alla geranga, haradat regga . . .

And PAUL *is clapping his hands and shouting.*

PAUL. No! No! No!

A moment's silence. PAUL *is tense. He knows he has to deliver his message.*

Set your minds on the higher gifts. Speaking in tongues is one of them. But I am going to put before you something better. For . . .

A beat.

Though I command languages both human and angelic – if I speak without love, I am no more than a gong booming or a cymbal clashing.

A beat.

And though I have the power of prophecy, to penetrate all mysteries and knowledge, and though I have all the faith necessary to move mountains – if I am without love, it will do me no good whatever.

A beat.

Love is always patient and kind; love is never jealous; love is not boastful or conceited, it is never rude and never seeks its own advantage, it does not take offence or store up grievances. Love does not rejoice at wrongdoing, but finds its joy in the truth. It is always ready to make allowances, to trust, to hope and endure whatever comes. Love never comes to an end. But if there are prophecies, they will be done away with; if tongues, they will fall silent; and if knowledge, it will be done away with. F . . .

A beat.

For we know only imperfectly, and we prophesy imperfectly; but once perfection comes, all imperfect things will be done away with. W . . . w . . . when I was a child, I used to talk like a child, and see things as a child does, and think like a child; but now that I have become an adult, I have finished with all childish ways.

A beat.

Now we see only reflections in a mirror, mere riddles, but then we shall be seeing face to face. Now, I can only know imperfectly; but then I shall know just as fully as I am myself known.

A beat.

As it is, these remain: faith, hope and love, the three of them; and the greatest of them is love.

A silence.

All are still. PAUL *and* BARNABAS *are looking at each other.*

1ST CORINTHIAN. Amen.

CORINTHIANS. Amen!

BARNABAS. Sing 'If we have died with Him'.

They sing in a canon. See hymn at 2 Timothy 2, 11-12.

ALL (*sing*).
If we have died with Him, we shall live with Him.
If we persevere, we shall reign with Him.

They finish. PAUL *and* BARNABAS *walk to each other and embrace.*

PAUL *returns to the prison scene.*

Scene Nine

Rome, AD 65. Prison. PAUL *and* PETER.

PETER. Yes. Your sermon on love at Corinth. When you wrote it out in a letter to the congregations, we were all moved. I wept.

PAUL. Well, there you have it. That truth was revealed to me, Peter. Directly, by the Holy Spirit, sent by Christ. He was with me in Corinth as He was with me on the Damascus road.

A beat.

PETER. I've lived with two things in my head.

PAUL. What do you mean?

PETER. Two truths, two Yeshuas, the man I knew and your Christ! It's my fault, my fault, I went along with it.

PAUL. Peter, what's the matter with you?

PETER. After you saw James in his house, when you came to stay with me . . .

PAUL. Wonderful days.

PETER. For me they were terrible.

PAUL. But you told me about being with Him, the life on the road, the arguments with priests, the faith of the people . . .

PETER. You don't know your strength, Paul. You never stand any contradiction. The force of your faith, it was a wave, drowning me. At the end of those fourteen days, I believed in everything you believed in. How does the mind do that? Believe two things at once!

PAUL. You're not making sense.

PETER. Paul, I have a terrible secret.

PAUL. Tell it to me.

PETER. I can't, it'll destroy you.

PAUL. Let's try to die in the full knowledge of our faith.

PETER *laughs, bitterly.*

PETER. 'The full knowledge of our faith.' (*To himself.*) What am I about to do?

A beat.

Very well.

A beat.

I was with you on the road to Damascus.

PAUL. You mean in spirit . . .

PETER. No, I was there! So was James. We were with Yeshua.

PAUL *stares at him.*

I argued against doing it to you but . . . I've never been the strongest.

PAUL. You were with Him on the road?

PETER. Yes. This is what happened.

PETER *stands, shedding his chains, and walks from the prison scene.*

This is the secret behind your 'truth'.

Scene Ten

Off the road to Damascus, AD 34.

Enter JAMES *and* PETER.

JAMES. Yeshua!

PETER. Yeshua!

JAMES. Yeshua!

PETER. Yeshua!

YESHUA *enters, stumbling then falling onto all fours, standing again.*

JAMES. There he is.

PETER. Rabbi!

They run toward YESHUA *who collapses.* JAMES *cradles him, pieta-like, in his arms.*

JAMES. Did you speak to him?

YESHUA *looks at* JAMES *without comprehension.*

Did you speak to Saul?

PETER. Rabbi, drink some water . . .

YESHUA *looks at* PETER. *He takes the water but passes out.* PETER *takes the water back.*

JAMES. Yeshua!

PETER. Let Him sleep. He could always sleep, that calm about Him.

JAMES. We must know what happened.

PETER. We shouldn't have made Him do this.

JAMES. It was his idea.

PETER. We shouldn't have let Him! Confronting a thug like Saul of Tarsus, alone out here, desperately dangerous.

JAMES. We are desperate.

PETER. Saul could have killed Him.

JAMES. He's been killed already. He's 'come back from the dead'. Haven't you, my beloved brother?

PETER. James . . .

JAMES *is bitterly upset.*

JAMES. My Holy brother. Never did anything simply. Always the ambiguous saying, the complex parable, the meaningful gesture. Washing the feet of prostitutes. Why did he have to wash the feet of so many of them? Even when he came to be crucified, did he hang there, scream and choke to death like any other religious rebel branded a criminal? No no. He had to survive.

PETER. He's my master, He's my teacher. I know He's your brother but you shouldn't talk about Him this way.

JAMES. Peter . . .

He collects himself.

I'm glad he survived, of course I am.

PETER. James, you know what people are beginning to believe. We must talk about it.

JAMES. I don't know if we dare.

PETER. When you showed Him to all the followers, nearly five hundred of us . . . so many did believe.

JAMES. It wasn't intended . . .

Hugging YESHUA.

Oh my brilliant brother, touched by God, you didn't want to preach this, did you?

He scoffs.

Resurrection.

PETER. That wonderful day when He stood there, showing us His wounds . . . for a moment I believed it.

JAMES. On no, not you!

PETER. I believed He rose from the dead.

JAMES. He survived his crucifixion!

PETER. But they speared His side.

JAMES. He didn't die!

PETER. The tomb was empty.

JAMES. He was never in the tomb!

PETER. The stone was moved.

JAMES. The stone was never moved because the tomb was never closed!

PETER. I know I know I know! But in my dreams I see it moved by an angel.

JAMES. Stones moved by angels . . . where do these stories come from, they get everywhere, poisoning minds.

PETER. God talks to us in stories. Stories are religion.

JAMES. Peter, I know the truth of my brother's so-called death and resurrection. You weren't there but I was, standing there on the execution ground in the rain.

PETER. I couldn't bear . . . no, I was frightened. I hid. I was so ashamed.

JAMES. We were all frightened and ashamed. He was a few feet away from me, hanging there, screaming, fighting for breath, screaming again.

They look at the unconscious YESHUA. *The pieta still holds.*

PETER. You should have let Him die.

JAMES. Yes. God forgive me, perhaps I should have.

PETER. You've never told me what actually happened.

JAMES *looks away.*

Of all people, I deserve to know.

JAMES. It was the rain. The centurion was bored with the execution. He decided to finish it. He ordered the guard to spear Yeshua in the side. I despaired. But when they took him down . . . he opened his eyes. Looked up at me. Out of the mud in that terrible place.

PETER. Maybe that was the miracle!

JAMES. No miracle, just someone with money. Joseph of Arimathea bribed the guards to say nothing. We wrapped Yeshua up and took him to Joseph's house. Smuggled him out of the city that night.

PETER. Never in the tomb.

JAMES. Never.

PETER. People have begun to die because they believe He was. Remember Stephen? He was the first. They say Saul was there, holding coats, when they stoned Him.

JAMES. Saul the demon, gloating, sucking at the last breath of the young martyr. He'll destroy all the followers.

YESHUA. Saul is dead.

A beat.

PETER. Rabbi . . .

YESHUA. Give me some water.

PETER *lifts the skin of water.*

JAMES. Yeshua . . .

YESHUA. Water.

PETER *helps* YESHUA *drink.*

PETER. You've got a fever.

YESHUA. It's the wound.

PETER (*to* JAMES). We must get Him back to the caves . . .

JAMES (*to* YESHUA). What do you mean, Saul is dead?

YESHUA. He's reborn.

JAMES *is horrified.*

JAMES. What did you say to him?

YESHUA. Only what he wanted to hear.

JAMES. That you rose from the dead?

YESHUA. All I said was that I am what he said I am.

JAMES (*to himself*). Why does this lie want to live?

YESHUA *is near fainting again and distressed.*

YESHUA. James, you tell me what I am, tell me, tell me.

PETER. We must go. I'll carry Him.

> PETER *goes to lift him but* YESHUA *has a rush of strength and grabs* JAMES.

YESHUA. Did God abandon me?

JAMES. No Yeshua, he's always been with you.

> PETER *walks into* . . .

Scene Eleven

Rome, AD 65. Prison. PAUL *and* PETER.

A silence.

PETER. You have to realise how desperate James was to stop you.

PAUL. It wasn't James who stopped me, it was the Lord.

PETER. Try to understand.

PAUL. There is nothing to understand. The risen Christ appeared to me.

PETER. You're blinding yourself.

PAUL. No, I was blinded on the road, by His glory.

PETER. You were persecuting us. That's why He confronted you.

PAUL. Yes, He did confront me! He asked me why I killed His followers. I couldn't answer, with Him standing there before me in the light.

PETER. What light?

PAUL. The light of His glory! The light of Heaven, that surrounds His Father.

PETER. There was no light. It was in your mind.

A beat. For a moment PAUL *hesitates.*

PAUL. In my mind.

PETER. The whole thing, in your mind.

PAUL. It's true I . . . had an attack.

PETER. You'd had a fit, that night, on the road?

PAUL. I was at my lowest, cut in half and He made me whole.

PETER. Paul, maybe your illness made it seem more than it was.

PAUL. What are you saying?

PETER. There was nothing mystical, nothing visionary about your meeting on the road.

PAUL. No! You're saying that Jesus was a kind of fever in my brain.

PETER. It was a desperate measure to stop your campaign. We were scattered to foreign countries or hiding in cellars, we couldn't preach, we could hardly meet. And now you were going out of Judea, to Damascus, where so many of us had fled.

PAUL. Why are you trying to make the Lord appearing to me sound like some kind of political trick . . .

PETER. Because it was! And it was Yeshua's idea. He took it on Himself to confront you, despite never having truly recovered from His wounds.

A beat.

So we let Him do it.

PAUL *is watchful, guarded, trying to deal with the information rushing at him.*

PAUL. You let Him?

PETER. Yes.

PAUL (*to himself*). Is the world . . . tilting sideways? Is truth sliding toward a precipice, falling into the darkness? (*To* PETER.) If . . . what you say is true, He survived . . .

PETER. Yes yes, that's it . . .

PAUL. Where was He hiding?

PETER. In the desert, the Qum'ran caves, with the Essenes.

PAUL. Those fanatics?

PETER. Paul, Yeshua did preach the truth. You met Him, you felt His strength. Even though He was a shadow of what He was before His ordeal, you couldn't withstand that mind. That purity. He was a great teacher, Paul, a great prophet. But He wasn't the son of God and He wasn't the Messiah. He was a man who suffered greatly for us, but a man.

A silence.

Then PAUL, *slowly, to himself.*

PAUL. He told me He had risen from the dead.

PETER. Did He? Are you sure?

PAUL. He showed me His wounds and told me He had risen from the dead.

PETER. Paul, think, did He say it, or did you want Him to say it?

PAUL. He asked me why I kicked against the truth.

PETER. Paul, you have got to listen to me . . .

PAUL. He told me the end of the world was coming.

PETER. But it hasn't.

PAUL. It will. In the twinkling of an eye. When we don't expect it. Jesus will return like a thief in the night.

PETER. He hasn't, Paul.

PAUL. This is blasphemy, Peter . . .

PETER. Fine fine, then I blaspheme! But look, I know you're
the theologian and I'm just a peasant fisherman, but I must
point out that after thirty years of day after day, even hour
after hour, preaching, praying, desperately trying to believe
that the world is about to end . . . nothing has happened.

PAUL. He told me!

PETER. Yeshua always wanted to provoke belief, not force it
on His hearers. Except with divorce: to that He always gave
a strong 'no'. Probably cos of his wife.

PAUL *flinches.*

He was a man, you know. Great, but just a man. I mean, we
all wanted Him to give her up. But He wouldn't. No, He
wouldn't admit He'd made a mistake. He was committed to
her and that was that. She was diseased, you know.

PAUL, *to himself, shaking his head.*

PAUL. No no no no.

PETER. But apart from His views on divorce . . . there was
always something . . . twisty in what He said. Someone in
crowd, a drunk, a fanatic or whatever, would say something
outrageous . . . even 'You're the Messiah' . . . and Yeshua
would reply, 'Is that what I am?' Always throw it back on
the questioner. Often people would laugh.

PAUL. 'Is that what I am?'

A beat.

But I saw Him again in Jerusalem!

PETER. Yes, we were hiding Him in James's house. There
were rows with the Essenes, they called Him 'the man of a
lie'. So we took Him at night to James's house. It was
dangerous but we were making arrangements to get Him out
of Judea.

PAUL. When do you say He died?

PETER. Ten years ago. In Syria. He's buried in a very secret
place.

A beat.

PAUL. No. This is wrong. No! Peter the rock, the slippery rock. I had to warn you once before, at Antioch, remember? You refused to eat with Gentiles.

PETER. I lost my way there . . .

PAUL. Haven't you again? With this wild story?

PETER. No!

PAUL. Peter the denier.

PETER. No!

PAUL. When faith goes, all kind of phantoms flare in the mind. Ignore them, keep on the thing before you: the clear picture of Jesus Christ crucified. Can't you see it, right in front of your eyes?

PETER. I'm trying to tell you the truth.

A beat.

PAUL. No. He appeared to me on the road to Damascus, He appeared to me again in Jerusalem.

PETER *is angry.*

PETER. Oh your second vision in Jerusalem. Do you know what was going on in Jerusalem? In the next room? We were working out how to never hear of you again.

PETER *walks from the prison into* . . .

Scene Twelve

Jerusalem, AD 37. YESHUA, MARY, JAMES *and* PETER.

YESHUA *sits on one side.* MARY *is at the back.*

JAMES. When the hotheads in the congregation know he's here, I won't be able to control them!

PETER. We must convince him to leave.

JAMES. Convince that lunatic?

PETER. We could tell him the truth.

JAMES. Then he'd return to persecuting us. And what propaganda he'd have, that we're liars, frauds . . . We brought this upon ourselves, I'm at a loss to know what to do.

YESHUA. Let him preach to the pagans.

They turn and look at YESHUA.

He'll take my teaching to the world.

PETER. No Rabbi, it's too risky . . .

YESHUA. God hasn't abandoned me. I won't abandon my apostle.

JAMES. He's not your apostle!

YESHUA. I have said he is.

JAMES. All I am trying to do is protect your teaching!

MARY *touches* YESHUA*'s hand.*

MARY. Why do any more? Why do anything? Why don't you just rest?

He leans forward and speaks to her intimately. JAMES *and* PETER *look away, embarrassed.*

YESHUA. I can't, Mary, because of what they think I am.

MARY. I hate what they think you are.

YESHUA. Don't blame them.

MARY. I have no life.

YESHUA. Nor do I.

MARY. What will happen to us?

YESHUA. We'll disappear into the stories they'll tell about us.

MARY. Lies.

YESHUA. Yes. But very beautiful lies. So beautiful in a way . . . they'll be true.

MARY *stares at* YESHUA *then lets go and looks away.*

For a moment it seems JAMES *is going to prevent* YESHUA *leaving the room but then he lets him pass.*

YESHUA *exits.*

PETER. Is He beginning to believe what Paul says about Him?

JAMES. I don't know but what matters is, this could be the solution. Paul will set off to preach around the Mediterranean and we'll never hear from him again.

PETER. I'm not so sure.

JAMES. Can you imagine an ugly man ranting about a crucified Jew being the Saviour of the world in Ephesus, Corinth, Athens, in Rome? They'll laugh at him. He'll be one more religious crank amongst hundreds. No, we'll send him on his 'mission' and never hear from him again. But first, take him to your house.

PETER. Please not. What'll we talk about over breakfast? Sin?

JAMES. He was impressed by you.

PETER. What if I end up agreeing with him?

JAMES. You have the tradition, you knew Yeshua when he was preaching. I think tradition matters to him, he yearns to be part of it. Tell him what Yeshua really said and did. Try to smooth his fanaticism. And we'll set a condition. He can travel with our authority if he collects money for us. He won't of course. Who'd give money to a lunatic preacher?

MARY. You won't stop it.

JAMES. Mary, yes?

MARY. It's what people want. They want a god, rising up in light, out of his grave! They want a figure shining in white, shooting up into the air! Angels and trumpets round his head! Whatever he really was or wasn't, it doesn't matter. My husband's disappearing. He's becoming a ghost and so am I. They want him to be God's son and how can God's son have slept with a whore, who has an Assyrian winged god tattooed on one buttock and Isis and the moon on the other? No no, he'll have to be pure. Oh a lot will have to change! Even his birth. I mean, how did his cow of a mother get pregnant?

JAMES. Stop this.

MARY. Oh come on! He's changing before our eyes into something called Jesus Christ, no earthly father for him, surely. God sent 'the word' and that impregnated the holy mother Mary, yeah. People will say God fucked her in the ear.

PETER. I . . .

JAMES. Be silent!

A beat.

MARY. I'll never be in the stories, not as his wife. I'll be some tart he made holy. On the edge. No face. No body.

Enter YESHUA.

YESHUA. Paul is ill.

JAMES *and* PETER *rush from the room.*

Scene Thirteen

Rome, AD 65. Prison. PAUL *and* PETER.

Anger has left PAUL. *He is calm, reflecting on what* PETER *has told him.*

PAUL. You thought I was a madman.

PETER. Deeply religious men can be deeply embarrassing.

PAUL. No no no. You saw me as crippled, in my mind.

PETER. What you call your thorn in the flesh, I . . .

PAUL. You think my ministry has been driven by my affliction?

PETER. James did, at first. But when he learnt of your success, and when you came back to Jerusalem fifteen years later, the leader of Christian communities throughout the Roman Empire, and with that huge sum of money . . . I don't know. I don't know what James thought. Yes I do. The way the story of your renamed Yeshua, your 'Jesus' spread like wildfire . . . he couldn't bear it. It killed him. I should have been with him when he died.

PAUL. But you weren't.

PETER. No.

PAUL. You were preaching what you call 'my' Jesus, with me.

PETER. Yes.

PAUL. Have you ever believed it?

PETER. I did for years.

PAUL. But now, hours before our death, you don't. And all that we've done, the people we've baptised, the congregations we've started . . . you say all that's a lie?

PETER *looks down, exhausted.*

Peter. Let your mind be filled with everything that is true, everything that is honourable, everything that is upright and pure, everything we love, with all that is good and worthy of praise.

PETER. Do you know you're quoting one of your sermons at me? That I have heard over and over and over again? Your force of will can't change what I know.

PAUL. The Holy Spirit will help you.

PETER. Yeshua didn't die on His cross.

PAUL *chants to reassure himself. He is in great distress.*

PAUL. Christ died for our sins, in accordance with the
scriptures, He was buried, on the third day He was raised to
life, in accordance with the scriptures, and He appeared to
Peter . . .

PETER. . . . No, it was a story . . .

PAUL *ignores* PETER*'s protests.*

PAUL. . . . and later to the twelve followers . . .

PETER. . . . true but they knew He didn't die . . .

PAUL. . . . and next He appeared to more than five hundred of
the brothers at the same time . . .

PETER. . . . a terrible mistake, they went mad, they
misunderstood . . .

PAUL. And then to James and then to all the apostles, last of
all He appeared to me too, me, the misshapen, the abnormal
child.

A beat. PAUL *is breathing heavily, near fainting.* PETER
tries to comfort him.

PETER. Paul . . .

PAUL *turns and blazes at him.*

PAUL. If Christ has not been raised then our preaching is
without substance. And so is our faith. If Christ has not
been raised our faith is pointless. And we have not been
freed from our sins. And all those who have died in Christ
are utterly lost.

PETER. So absolute!

PAUL. It is absolute!

PETER. The teachings are good, there's a kindness in them,
they have an everydayness . . . isn't it enough that they tell
us, simply, how to live?

PAUL. No. If our faith in Christ is only about this life, then what are we? Deluded, pitiful creatures. If He did not rise then we are liars and there is no point to us or to life. All we could say is eat, get drunk, for tomorrow we die.

PETER. Forgive me.

PAUL. For what?

PETER. For killing the great story.

PAUL. If it was never true then it was never alive.

PETER. No.

Enter the CHIEF GAOLER *with others.*

CHIEF GUARD. Now your visitor is here. And there are rules of behaviour. You lie on your faces. Do it!

The other GAOLERS *force* PETER *and* PAUL *to lie on their stomachs.*

If you are invited to stand, you do not, you stay on all fours. And you do not look at him. And you do not make any movement toward him at all. Got that?

A beat.

Got that!

PAUL. Yes!

PETER. Yes!

CHIEF GAOLER (*close*). If there is any incident at all, my skin will be flayed but that will be nothing to what will happen to you. We could delay your executions for a week of tortures. So. Sensible behaviour please.

PETER. Who is it, who is coming?

CHIEF GAOLER. Nero Claudius Caesar, Emperor of the world.

They step back.

Enter NERO. *He is magnificently dressed and is wearing the mask of a woman's face.*

NERO. Or Emperor of the known world. Because there must be others, must there not? I mean, this shit-hole existence can't be all there is. What do you think, Christians? Are there other worlds for me to rule? You may stand.

The GAOLERS *are vigilant.* PAUL *and* PETER *raise themselves on all fours.*

Which one of you is the Roman citizen?

PAUL. I am.

CHIEF GAOLER. I am, Caesar!

NERO (*to the* CHIEF GAOLER). Leave us.

CHIEF GAOLER. Caesar I . . .

NERO. If they kill me it will be a whimsical death. But power is such a whimsical thing.

A gesture from NERO. *The* GAOLERS *withdraw.*

Did I condemn you in my court?

PAUL. Yes.

NERO. I don't remember. I expect I was drunk.

PAUL. I asked to be crucified.

NERO. Like your god, ah. The clerk of the court said no of course.

PAUL. Yes.

NERO (*to* PETER). But you are to be nailed up?

PETER *is terrified.*

PETER. Yes, Caesar.

NERO. Good good, so we are clear. You are both in effect dead men. That's why I'm here. I like to talk to the dead. Only they can keep my secrets.

He takes off his mask revealing an exhausted face.

Don't . . . kneel there like dogs, please. These little humiliations, these rituals. I know they maintain power. Along with the fear.

PAUL *and* PETER *sit back.*

Rituals. Repeated patterns of behaviour. To shore up belief. To stop chaotic behaviour. In the end it is the ritual that matters in religion, not what it means, mm? Like you imagining you're drinking the blood of a dead god?

PAUL *about to say something.*

No no, I am aware you don't kill babies, imperial spies have been to your ritual of the last supper.

PAUL. Spies?

NERO. Oh yes. You have long been seen as a political danger to the Imperial State.

PAUL. You persecute us because we threaten your gods.

NERO. You don't threaten our gods, what are you talking about, man?

A glance away and he lowers his voice.

Our gods don't exist. And I speak as someone who will be made into one when I'm dead. It's happened to most of my family, even Claudius. No, the threat from you is political.

PAUL. We are not a political threat.

NERO. Oh you are. You do know your so-called congregations have always been riddled with informers?

PAUL. No.

NERO. No?

NERO *laughs.*

PAUL. Why do you think we are a threat?

NERO. Because you're leaders of a death cult. Death cults
   always give the state problems. We don't like them.
   Mithras, well, that we're getting to grips with. The Eleusian
   mysteries in Greece, Rome has never liked: Persephone into
   the underworld, reborn in the spring. Not good. Too
   secretive, too personal. But there's only one ceremony every
   year and we have learnt to police it. Bribing priests usually
   works. But for now you don't have priests you have
   'apostles', appointed only by crazed visions of 'faith', the
   'Holy Spirit' . . .

PETER *is startled.*

PETER. You know . . .

NERO. Yes yes, Jew, I know a lot about Christianity. I am an
   artist after all. Only an artist can really understand religion.

PAUL. Christianity is not a threat to the Empire.

NERO. You thought it was before you changed names. And
   sides.

PAUL. The Kingdom of God was never to be a rebellion in
   Judea. I stopped that nonsense. The Kingdom of God is not
   of this world.

NERO. Yes, you have made some theological progress. You've
   laid the grounds to make your cult acceptable. And you
   probably do sense what its future could be.

PAUL. There is no future. Christ is about to return.

NERO. Oh please! I'm talking to the most intelligent dead
   man I've got hold of for years . . . don't spoil it with
   mumbo-jumbo. Listen. A state secret for the dead to take to
   their graves. In the next few years, Rome will destroy
   Judea.

PETER. Destroy?

NERO. We will flatten your country, Jew. Disarm and execute
   all the militias. All the fanatics on the roads, in the deserts.
   But not just the lunatics on the fringe. We will destroy all
   the priests, your Pharasees, your Sadducees, your

Maccabeans. Then we will tear down the Jerusalem Temple, we won't leave a stone upon a stone. It will be so beautiful, like a song.

PETER. Destroy the Temple . . .

NERO. Destroy the whole country. It will no longer exist.

PETER. This is a . . . prophesy?

NERO. No, it's a well-advanced military plan. You won't be able to shout out about it tomorrow, you know, you'll have your tongues cut out.

A silence.

PAUL. Christ will come any day now . . .

NERO. He won't. And you know it. But look: when Judea is destroyed, your cult will have its chance. It can cut itself off from its Jewish roots, leave all that garbage about the Law of Moses behind. And basically your teaching is fine: it's quietist, it's authoritarian, its views on divorce are socially stabilising, it stresses respectful behaviour, particularly amongst women. And when you have priests, Antioch, Corinth, Byzantium, Ephesus and Rome, above all Rome . . . a good hierarchy of bribable gentlemen in fine robes, like any other religion . . . Why, then you will do business with the state. A hundred, two hundred years from now, Christianity could be the Empire's official religion.

PAUL. Then why not release us now?

NERO. No no no, have you understood nothing? History needs your story. First the martyrdoms, the diaspora, the despair, then the full flowering of myth and poetry.

Smiles.

You only preach two things, Paul: resurrection and the end of the world. Hardly any story at all! Christianity will need much more than that. But history will embellish: you as saints, me as one of the worst singers who ever lived. History is all lies. Goodnight gentlemen.

He turns away.

PAUL. Creature of darkness. Man of despair. Demon-ridden man. Godless. Lost. Listen to me.

NERO *turns back to him.*

I believe Jesus died on the cross and rose again on the third day, to save us from our sins. And that at any moment He will return in glory and we will be counted.

NERO. Counted?

PAUL. It's not too late even for you to be saved, Caesar.

NERO *leans close to* PAUL.

NERO. Pedlar of illusions. Man of false teachings. Ridden with a false god. Lost. You listen to me. We are mud. And to mud we will return. We all secretly know it and it's our glory.

PAUL. I'll pray for you.

A beat. They are staring at each other.

Then suddenly NERO *turns on* PETER.

NERO. What about you? You're silent. Do you believe . . .

Satirically, sing-song.

. . . they stuck him up and pulled him down and up he popped from the grave and now he's on the right hand of God and watch out, humankind! He's coming back, any day now, to burn your backsides off if you're not on your knees? Hunh?

A silence.

Well? Do you believe it?

A silence.

PETER. Yes.

He looks at PAUL.

Christ died for my sins and rose from the dead.

NERO. The poetry of delusion is so strong.

He is about to go.

PETER. When I die tomorrow I don't want to be crucified like Him.

NERO. Oh don't start begging and gibbering for your life, you were doing so well.

PETER. No. Not the way He was. I'm not worthy. Crucify me upside down.

NERO *looks at him. Then shrugs.*

NERO. If that's your fancy.

And he holds the mask up to his face. They stare at each other for a moment.

Exit NERO.

A silence.

PAUL. Peter.

PETER. They'll tear our tongues out.

PAUL. Peter.

PETER. Do that too.

PAUL. Peter.

PETER. I lied to him.

PAUL. No.

PETER. I couldn't . . . tell that thing who came here . . . it was a lie.

PAUL. It's not.

PETER. I couldn't tell him the truth.

PAUL. You did.

PETER. Yeshua is buried in Syria. In a place called . . .

PAUL. No, no, hush hush.

PETER. He didn't rise . . .

PAUL. Hush.

PETER. What have we done?

PAUL. Just say it.

PETER. No.

PAUL. Say it. And believe it.

PETER. I can't. I can't.

PAUL. Say it, my brother, my fellow apostle, first father of the Roman congregation. Say it.

A beat.

Low to a crescendo.

PETER. Christ is risen.

PAUL. Christ is risen.

PETER. Christ is risen.

PAUL. Christ is risen.

PETER. Christ is risen.

PAUL. Christ is risen.

PETER. Christ is risen.

PAUL. Christ is risen.

PETER. Christ is risen.

PAUL. Christ is risen.

PETER. Christ is risen.

PAUL. Christ is risen.

PETER. Christ is risen.

PAUL. Christ is risen.

PETER. Christ is risen.

PAUL. Christ is risen.

PETER. Christ is risen.

PAUL. Christ is risen.

PETER. Christ is risen.

PAUL. Christ is risen.

PETER. Christ is risen.

PAUL. Christ is risen.

PETER. Christ is risen.

PAUL. Christ is risen.

PETER. Christ is risen.

PAUL. Christ is risen.

PETER. Christ is risen.

PAUL. Christ is risen.

PETER. Christ is risen.

PAUL. Christ is risen.

PETER. Christ is risen.

PAUL. Christ is risen.

PETER. Christ is risen.

PAUL. Christ is . . .

A blackout.

End.